WHAT WILL HAPPEN TO MY KIDS?

ESTATE PLANNING AS AN ACT OF TRUE LOVE

CINDY M. KANG, ESQ.

CMK
LAW GROUP

Mighty Seniors Publishing.

Paperback ISBN: 978-1-959833-04-8

e-Book ISBN: 978-1-959833-05-5

Dedicated to my most precious sons, Matthew, Ryan, and Nicky.

Thank you for making my life feel so full and for lighting up my life every day.

I love you forever. Love, Mommy

CONTENTS

INTRODUCTION

When my first son was born, I realized that a piece of me would live on forever. Amid the typical concerns of a new parent, from daily care needs to dreams about his bright future, I found myself pondering what might happen to him if, God forbid, something were to happen to me and my husband suddenly. In the unfortunate event of an accident, who would care for this little, helpless being we cherished so much? It dawned on me that, as a mother, the choices and actions I make today will directly impact my son's well-being and resonate through future generations. It served as both a weighty realization and a crucial wake-up call, compelling me to carefully consider and plan, striving to be the most responsible and loving parent I could be.

While many of us avoid contemplating our demise, secretly hoping for a death cure, the undeniable truth is that one day, it will happen to all of us. People often plan for unlikely scenarios like fires, with designated family meeting spots, and even stockpile emergency supplies for apocalyptic scenarios. However, what often gets overlooked are the certainties – our lives and eventual deaths. This book aims to underscore the importance of planning for these certainties and dispelling the taboo around discussing and openly facing these crucial end-of-life plans.

It's a common misconception that many people believe they don't have a will or other estate plan in place. In reality, without your own will or trust, the government default rules will dictate how your assets get distributed and who will care for your minor children after your passing. If establishing a will or trust feels daunting, the reality of what may happen when leaving these matters to the government can be truly terrifying.

By neglecting your estate plans, you inadvertently let the government take charge. They may compel your children to live with people you'd never want them to associate with, and they will seize as much of your money as they see fit to settle your affairs. This book aims to empower you with the knowledge to retain control over what happens to your kids and assets throughout your life and after your passing.

You will find the invaluable information in this book helpful, encouraging you to prepare your legal documents for genuine peace of mind, knowing you've fulfilled your role as a responsible parent to the best of your ability.

To Your Peace of Mind,

Cindy M. Kang, Esq.

1

THE UNSPOKEN CONCERN

I hope to facilitate an open and honest exploration of the often-dreaded topic of death planning and the frequently underestimated repercussions of passing away without a will or trust in place. I'm not just speaking from my point of view as an estate planning lawyer; I also understand the shared concerns and responsibilities that accompany parenthood and caring for aging parents.

Joyous moments and significant milestones naturally take the spotlight in raising a family. Nevertheless, it's crucial to recognize the unspoken concern that quietly lingers in the background: What if, unexpectedly, we're no longer there for our children? It's a thought that many parents, myself included, have grappled with.

The pages in this book are designed to provide a safe space for navigating the complexities of this concern. There is no denial or sugarcoating, but rather an open conversation about the emotional and practical aspects of securing your children's future. Because, let's face it, being a parent is a rollercoaster of emotions, and discussing the tough stuff is vital (albeit challenging).

Avoidance won't make these concerns vanish; it might amplify them. By addressing these questions head-on, we're not only being responsible parents but also actively participating in shaping a more secure future for our loved ones.

So, let's embark on a brief yet crucial exploration that goes beyond legalities. We're delving into the heart of responsible parenting—one that values emotional and practical security just as much as financial planning. Together, let's navigate the uncharted waters and understand why having an estate plan is a fundamental aspect of nurturing the well-being of our children.

2

THE IMPACT ON YOUR KIDS

Let's delve into the profound implications of not having a solid estate plan for your children.

Picture this scenario:

You and your spouse have built a great life together. Your sons, Alex and Max, radiate joy in your world—thoughtful, funny, and affectionate. Alex loves soccer, dinosaurs, and origami, while Max, with his playful sense of humor, enjoys tiptoeing around the house, ready to scare his next unsuspecting victim with a big "boo!" The pure joy in his laughter is contagious.

As diligent parents with demanding careers, you sought assistance in childcare. After an extensive search, you found the perfect nanny, Taylor, who is bilingual, reliable, and adored by Alex and Max. She handles household tasks and nurtures your children with patience and care.

You decide to take the kids on a weekend trip to a nearby beach town an hour away to stay at a beautiful short-term rental when your spouse will be out of town for an international business trip.

You bring Taylor along to help you with the kids, so you can also attend a two-hour yoga workshop on Saturday at the beach a few miles away from the rental. You decide to jog there and tell Taylor you're leaving your cell phone and wallet at home since you'll be nearby and back soon. After a great yoga and meditation session, you take a brief detour on your way back to buy frozen yogurt for the kids and Taylor.

On your way to the yogurt shop, tragedy strikes. An unexpected motorcyclist suddenly hits a curb right next to you, spins out of control, and takes your life instantly.

The unforeseen disaster leaves Taylor unaware, and without any means of identification on you, the paramedics who arrive at the scene have no idea who to notify. Taylor is wondering what could be taking you so long to return. She starts to worry, especially because she knows you don't have your phone or ID.

As the hours pass, Taylor's concern intensifies. Panic sets in as Taylor attempts to call your spouse, who is on an airplane for the next 12 hours. She grapples with the decision—should she involve the police or seek help elsewhere? The fate of your children hangs in the balance.

Without a plan, Taylor does not know the steps to take when tragedy strikes and has no choice but to call the police. When the police arrive, Taylor is told that she does not have the legal authority to keep your children as she could not show them any legal documents stating so.

Despite her pleas, the officer informs Taylor that Child Protective Services will take over until authorities locate you, your spouse, or another family member. Unfamiliar with Taylor, the police and social worker insist she leaves, placing Alex and Max in temporary foster care.

Alex and Max are sent to stay with a foster family. They endure a frightening and confusing experience with the foster family and their three older foster siblings, who appear to have a mixture of anger and substance abuse problems. The unfamiliar and terrifying foster care experience leaves lasting scars, affecting both Alex and Max's ability to trust people for many years after that.

When your spouse finally learns of the tragedy and returns home, he comes home to two completely different children he had left just a few days earlier. They are heartbroken and traumatized by the foster care siblings who interacted inappropriately with them during their night at the foster home. It takes years of counseling and therapy to get the kids to fully open up about their internalized trauma.

This heartbreaking scenario is a risk that millions of people face each day without an appropriate estate plan in place.

The emotional journey your children would face without proper planning is significant. From the uncertainty about their living arrangements to the potential disruption of their daily lives, the profound impact of such instability on their emotional well-being would be considerable.

Beyond emotions, there are practical challenges to anticipate. Without clear guidance, questions about schooling, medical care, and day-to-day routines can become uncharted territory for your children. How can we prevent this unthinkable situation from happening to our most treasured children?

Navigating Guardianship Issues Amidst Uncertainty

Central to the discussion is the issue of guardianship, which is the process of designating a person to care for your minor children or dependents in case of incapacity or death. Without a designated plan, the fate of your children would be unclear, potentially leading to lengthy family conflicts in court over who should step in while your children hang in the balance.

Understanding the complexities of guardianship is vital. Designating both temporary and permanent guardians requires careful planning and ensures your children are placed in a familiar and secure environment, minimizing disruptions during an already devastating and challenging time.

By proactively planning and documenting the guardianship process ahead of time, you are actively mitigating unnecessary stress and risk for your children and safeguarding their well-being.

Let's see what an alternate ending might look like to Alex and Max's story after losing their parent during that fateful weekend...

You and your spouse have been thorough. When Alex was born, you met with an estate planning attorney who helped you prepare a comprehensive Children's Protection Package, providing instructions to caretakers in case of an emergency.

Janice, your best friend who lives 15 minutes from your home, is the first on the list. She immediately drives out to the short-term rental as soon as your nanny, Taylor, calls her when you never return from your walk.

Having a copy of the document giving her legal authority as the kids' guardian, Janice ensures your kids won't be taken into foster care. Taylor and Janice call the police, who are relieved to find documented legal authority. Your kids remain with Janice while the police investigate your disappearance. They discover you have died.

The children are devastated, but at least they are in the care of loving and familiar people while they wait for your spouse to return home.

Upon your spouse's return, and following your funeral services, your children and spouse all go to family counseling together to fully work through the grieving process of losing you. It is difficult, but at least they have each other and had the comfort of Janice and Taylor while your spouse was away during the most difficult days.

What a difference a few sheets of paper can make in the lives of your most treasured loved ones in the event of your untimely passing.

3

DISPELLING MYTHS AND FEARS

Estate planning often carries an air of complexity and mystery, leading to widespread misconceptions. Let's address some of the most common misunderstandings, breaking complex notions into manageable concepts.

Myth #1: Estate Planning is Only for the Wealthy

One prevalent myth is that estate planning is exclusively for the wealthy. Here, we debunk this notion and emphasize how estate planning is a valuable tool for individuals and families of varying financial backgrounds. It's about securing your loved ones' future, regardless of your income.

Estate planning addresses the distribution of assets, whether they're worth $50,000, $500,000, or $5 million, and determines who can make crucial decisions regarding your finances and medical matters in the event of incapacitation. Doing so helps avoid the expensive and time-consuming probate process, ensuring a smoother transition for your family during already challenging times.

~

Myth #2: I'm Too Young for Estate Planning

Another misconception revolves around age. There may be better strategies than waiting until a later stage in life, as there are compelling reasons to start the estate planning process early.

By initiating this process sooner, individuals can address critical matters, such as authorizing a trusted person to make important financial and medical decisions if they cannot make those decisions themselves. This proactive approach ensures a smoother and more secure future, regardless of age.

~

Myth #3: It's Complicated and Time-Consuming

Many people believe estate planning is complex and time-consuming, causing them to put it off. However, the reality is that with the guidance of a qualified estate planning attorney, the process can be streamlined and tailored to individual needs. Dispelling the myth that it's overly complicated can motivate individuals to take the necessary steps to get their affairs in order.

Moreover, modern estate planning tools leverage technology to simplify the process further. Online client portals, Zoom client calls, and digital secure signing platforms make it easier than ever to gather information and collaborate with attorneys who are experts in the law and technology forward. With user-friendly interfaces and step-by-step guidance, the complexity often associated with estate planning dissolves with the proper professional support.

By embracing these advancements, individuals can confidently navigate the estate planning process, addressing their unique concerns efficiently and often without even needing to leave their homes or offices. These advancements showcase how accessible and adaptable estate planning has become in today's digital age.

Myth #4: DIY Estate Planning is a Cost-Effective Shortcut

There's a prevailing belief that opting for do-it-yourself (DIY) estate planning solutions, such as those provided by platforms like LegalZoom, is more economical and straightforward than consulting an estate planning lawyer. While the initial costs of these DIY services may appear attractive, the potential downsides and enduring consequences can far outweigh any perceived savings. (Full Disclosure: my family happens to be good friends with the co-founder of LegalZoom, and I'm not in any way disparaging the company; I'm just clarifying that their services and the services provided by an actual estate attorney are two very different services!)

These online platforms often offer generic, one-size-fits-all templates that may not adequately address the unique complexities of individual situations. Estate planning demands a nuanced understanding of legal intricacies and personal circumstances. A qualified estate planning attorney brings expertise to tailor solutions to your needs, ensuring your plan aligns with your goals and considers any potential complexities.

The apparent simplicity of DIY solutions can lead to critical errors, as legal documents are precise instruments where minor mistakes can have significant repercussions. With their knowledge and experience, estate planning attorneys can navigate potential pitfalls, preventing costly legal battles and family disputes. Opting for a qualified attorney is an investment in your affairs' long-term security and clarity, offering personalized guidance and legal insight that generic templates cannot provide.

4

DECODING ESSENTIAL ESTATE PLANNING TERMS

Embarking on the estate planning journey necessitates demystifying legal jargon. Let's cover some key terms as a starting point.

Wills vs Trusts

A Last Will and Testament (also known as "Wills") is a basic directive for estate asset distribution and guardianship. While a will is certainly better than nothing, it often exposes loved ones to an expensive and lengthy probate process. It also only covers what happens in case of death but does not address the event of incapacity.

Trusts provide a flexible, private, and probate-avoidant solution. With trusts, you can tailor your estate plan to your specific needs and preferences, offering comprehensive protection for your assets during life and potential incapacity. Living Trusts are trusts created during an individual's lifetime that can be used to manage and distribute assets.

Legal Jargon Demystified

General Estate Planning Terms

Estate: The total property a person owns, both tangible and intangible.

Estate Plan: An estate plan is a comprehensive strategy outlining the management and distribution of a person's assets, as well as specifying their wishes regarding medical decisions, guardianship, and other important matters, in the event of incapacity or death.

Estate Tax: Taxes imposed on transferring an individual's property upon their death, regardless of whether they died with or without a will or trust.

Intestate: Dying without a valid will or trust, resulting in the state determining the distribution of assets.

Incapacity: A state where an individual cannot make decisions for themselves, often due to illness or disability.

Terms Generally Related to Wills

Probate: The legal process through which a deceased person's will is validated and their estate is administered.

Executor: A person designated in a will to carry out the deceased person's wishes and manage the estate during probate.

Guardianship: The legal appointment of a guardian to make decisions for minor children or incapacitated adults. Note: In California, "conservatorship" is commonly used instead of "guardianship" when making decisions for incapacitated adults. The terminology may vary by jurisdiction; different states use different terms to describe similar legal concepts.

Codicil: An amendment or addition to a will.

Heirs are individuals designated by law to inherit the assets of a deceased person who did not leave a valid will.

Terms Generally Related to Trusts

Trustee: A trustee is an individual or entity appointed to oversee and manage the assets and affairs of a trust by the trust document and for the benefit of its beneficiaries.

Beneficiary: A beneficiary is an individual or entity named in a will, trust, or insurance policy to receive specific assets or benefits.

Other Estate Planning Documents

Power of Attorney: A legal document that grants someone the authority to make decisions on behalf of another person.

Durable Power of Attorney: "Durable" signifies that the power of attorney endures even if you become incapacitated.

Living Will: Not to be confused with a Last Will and Testament. A living will is a document that outlines an individual's preferences for medical treatment if they become unable to communicate. It often addresses issues such as life-sustaining treatments, organ donation, and end-of-life care preferences.

Healthcare Proxy: This legal document appoints a healthcare agent authorized to make medical decisions on the individual's behalf if they become unable to do so, ensuring their healthcare preferences are respected and followed.

Advance Healthcare Directive: This term is commonly used in many states, including California, to refer to a legal document combining elements of a Living Will and a Healthcare Proxy. However, the specific terminology may vary by state, and other terms like "Healthcare Power of Attorney," "Medical Power of Attorney," or "Directive to Physicians" may be used in different jurisdictions to describe similar documents. It's essential to use the terminology and formalities that align with the legal requirements and practices in your state to be legally valid.

Estate vs Net Worth

"Estate" and "net worth" are related concepts but are not the same. Here's the distinction:

Estate: The term "estate" typically refers to the total assets and liabilities of an individual at a specific point in time, encompassing both financial and non-financial assets. It includes real estate, personal property, investments, debts, and other possessions. In estate planning, the focus is often on how these assets will be managed or distributed upon the individual's death.

Net Worth: Net worth, on the other hand, is a financial metric representing the difference between an individual's assets and liabilities. It's a measure of an individual's wealth, calculated by subtracting debts and other obligations from the total value of assets. Net worth provides a snapshot of financial health and can be positive or negative.

While "estate" encompasses a broader range of assets and liabilities, "net worth" refers explicitly to an individual's financial standing by calculating the difference between their assets and liabilities.

Crafting Your Legacy

"Legacy" refers to the lasting impact, influence, or contributions an individual leaves behind, often extending beyond their lifetime. It encompasses the values, beliefs, accomplishments, and memories that shape how they are remembered and their impact on future generations.

In estate planning, legacy can involve considerations beyond financial assets, including the intangible aspects of a person's life that they wish to pass on to their heirs.

Estate planning is akin to storytelling—a narrative that goes beyond legalities. It captures who you are, weaving a tale that resonates across generations. Your legacy extends beyond wealth to the intangibles, reflecting the wisdom gained, values upheld and shared love.

As you navigate estate planning, consider the values, stories, and experiences that have shaped you. It's not just about arranging assets but crafting a timeless legacy that speaks to the heart and soul of your family.

Holistic Protection

Estate planning is your comprehensive shield beyond securing your financial stability and designating guardians for your children. It's not just about numbers; it's about creating a lasting legacy and ensuring the well-being of your loved ones during times of incapacity and beyond. Those who take action today can shape the narrative of their legacy and shield their family's future.

5

IF YOU DON'T DECIDE WHAT SHOULD HAPPEN, THE GOVERNMENT WILL

What would happen to your kids and your assets if you were to die without a will or trust? What government rules would govern how your assets are distributed and how your children would be looked after? Are these things you should know?

Each state has specific laws governing these scenarios, outlining default procedures that may not align with your wishes. It's essential to be aware of these laws to appreciate the potential consequences of needing a plan in place.

Here are just a few of the risks associated with dying intestate and having your loved ones subjected to your state's default probate rules:

Foster Care for Your Children

One significant risk of dying intestate is the uncertainty surrounding the guardianship of your minor children. Without a designated legal guardian in your estate plan, the court may have to appoint someone, and this process can result in temporary or, in some cases, permanent foster care for your children. Taking proactive steps to designate a guardian ensures your children's well-being and clarifies unforeseen circumstances.

Family Conflicts and Disputes

Relying on the state's default probate plan may lead to family conflicts over asset distribution and guardianship decisions. Without a personalized estate plan, family members may have different expectations, potentially resulting in disputes that can strain relationships.

Financial Implications and Delays

The probate process can be lengthy and expensive. The default plan may not optimize finances, resulting in unnecessary expenses and complications. This can lead to delays in settling the estate, causing financial strain for heirs and beneficiaries.

Lack of Personalization

The default plan does not account for each family's unique dynamics and priorities. Without personalization, the distribution of assets and guardianship decisions may not align with the individual wishes of the deceased, potentially impacting the well-being of surviving family members.

Addressing these risks through proactive estate planning allows individuals to tailor their strategies, minimize conflicts, streamline the process, and precisely meet their intentions.

6

TAILORING YOUR ESTATE PLAN FOR YOUR FAMILY

The previous chapters discussed some risks and pitfalls of dying without a plan. Now, let's review what your journey to craft a personalized estate plan tailored to the unique needs of your family would entail.

Understanding Your Family's Dynamics

Before diving into the legal aspects, take a moment to reflect on your family's dynamics. Consider your family's values, aspirations, and individual needs. Understanding these dynamics lays the foundation for a comprehensive estate plan reflecting your intentions.

Identifying Your Priorities

Delve into what matters most to you. Whether it's ensuring financial security for your children, preserving family traditions, or supporting charitable causes, identifying your priorities helps shape the critical elements of your estate plan.

Choosing the Right Guardian

Building on the discussion from previous chapters, explore the criteria for choosing a guardian precisely aligned with your family dynamics. This decision is central to the well-being and upbringing of your children.

Streamlining Asset Distribution

You will want to explore strategies with an estate planning expert to minimize delays and complications in asset distribution. This exploration involves considering options like revocable living trusts, how to title real estate assets, and other mechanisms to expedite the transfer of assets.

Community Property Considerations

For married couples, community property rules in states like California play a significant role. Your estate planning professionals can confirm if you are in a community property state and if so, can unpack the implications of these rules on asset distribution and help craft strategies to optimize the handling of community property within your estate plan.

Tax Planning

Each state has its own set of tax considerations regarding estate planning. You will want a solid understanding of trust and estate taxes specific to your state to take advantage of potential tax-saving strategies.

Healthcare Directives and End-of-Life Decision-Making

Healthcare Directives within the estate planning landscape are crucial to put you in control of your medical decisions if you cannot make those decisions yourself due to incapacity. Having a legally valid Advance Healthcare Directive and other legal documents, such as a valid HIPAA medical release form, provides peace of mind for you and your loved ones.

Durable Power of Attorney for Financial Matters

A Durable Power of Attorney for Financial Matters is equally vital within the estate planning framework. This legal document empowers a trusted individual to manage your financial affairs in case of your incapacity. With a Durable Power of Attorney, you designate someone to handle financial decisions on your behalf, offering a comprehensive approach to safeguarding your interests during times of incapacity.

The combination of a well-crafted Durable Power of Attorney for Financial Matters and healthcare directives provides comprehensive protection, not only for your medical well-being but also for the prudent management of your financial affairs. This proactive approach offers invaluable reassurance to both you and your loved ones, ensuring a seamless and secure transition in managing your personal and financial matters when needed most.

7

LEGAL GUIDANCE AND ENSURING ON-GOING PLAN EFFECTIVENESS

Navigating the intricate landscape of estate planning requires the expertise of a qualified professional. In this chapter, let's discuss the pivotal role of a seasoned estate planning expert to ensure your estate plan documents are legally valid and work correctly when your family's future depends on them.

Don't Skimp on Something This Important

With something as important as who will look after your children and all of your assets, we cannot overemphasize the importance of seeking counsel from a qualified estate planning attorney with specialized knowledge of estate planning law. Their expertise can guide you through the intricacies of the legal framework, ensuring your plan aligns seamlessly with your wishes and is in compliance with applicable laws and regulations.

Regularly Reviewing Your Plan for Continued Relevance

Estate planning is not a "one-and-done" affair. Instead, it is critical to have ongoing periodic reviews of your estate plan to guarantee its continued relevance. Consider the dynamic nature of circumstances, changing family dynamics, and evolving laws. Regular reviews guided by a seasoned attorney, usually every few years or when there's a significant change in your life (such as the birth of a new child), ensure that your plan remains effective and adaptable to the shifts in your life.

Choose an Attorney You Can Relate To

Since your estate planning attorney will potentially become your family's long-term trusted advisor, you want to select someone you feel completely comfortable with, actually like (hey, not all of us attorneys are corporate stiffs!), and can trust and rely on.

8

SAFEGUARDING YOUR CHILDREN'S FUTURE

Let's shed more light on the legal processes and real-life consequences that may arise if parents pass away without a clear estate plan.

Children's Protective Services (CPS) Involvement

Every state in the United States has its agency responsible for child protective services, although these agencies' specific names and structures may vary by state. These agencies ensure children's safety and well-being in various situations, including when their legal guardians cannot care for them.

In California, when parents haven't specified guardianship arrangements and unforeseen circumstances arise, Children's Protective Services (CPS) may intervene to ensure the children's immediate well-being. CPS assesses the situation, providing the children are placed in a safe and stable environment.

However, this intervention can lead to temporary foster care if suitable family members or friends with legal authority are unavailable immediately.

Proactively designating a legal guardian in your estate plan mitigates the need for CPS involvement, providing a more secure and familiar environment for your children in challenging times.

Temporary Placement in Foster Care

In the absence of immediate family members or a designated guardian, children may be placed in temporary foster care. This transition can have profound emotional and psychological effects on children as they navigate unfamiliar environments and relationships. The sudden upheaval disrupts their sense of security and stability, leaving lasting impressions that may affect their trust in others.

Navigating the Court Appointment Process

When parents still need to designate guardians for their children, the legal processes initiated by the court come into play. The timeline for appointing a legal guardian involves a series of court hearings and evaluations to determine the most suitable candidate. Factors such as the prospective guardian's relationship with the children, stability, and ability to provide a nurturing environment are carefully considered.

Potential Delays and Uncertainties

The court appointment process for legal guardianship can introduce significant delays and uncertainties. The timeline for court decisions, often subject to various factors and stakeholders, may prolong the period of uncertainty for your children. This delay can impact their emotional well-being, creating a sense of instability during an already stressful time.

In essence, embracing estate planning is an empowering act that places parents in the driver's seat of their children's future. By making informed decisions and crafting a comprehensive plan, parents protect their assets and, more importantly, safeguard the well-being and stability of their children.

Parents are urged to embark on their estate planning journey, ensuring a secure and tailored framework that reflects their values and priorities. In taking this proactive step, parents affirm their commitment to providing a stable and protected environment for their loved ones, both now and in the future.

CONCLUSION

As we reach the end of our journey together through the basics of estate planning and how its lack thereof can impact our children, it's essential to reflect on the insights you gained along the way. We began with "The Unspoken Concern," unraveling the importance of facing the inevitable with preparedness. Chapter 2 vividly illustrated the potential repercussions on our children when the safety net of an estate plan is absent—a scenario we wouldn't wish upon anyone.

In "Dispelling Myths and Fears," we confronted common misconceptions, paving the way for informed decisions. "Decoding Essential Terms" empowered us with the language to navigate this intricate landscape. Chapter 5 urged us to ponder a crucial question: "Do you want the government's plan to control your assets and children?" The subsequent chapters guided us in tailoring a plan for our unique families, emphasizing legal guidance and ongoing plan effectiveness.

As we stand on the threshold of "Safeguarding Your Children's Future," the gravity of these decisions resonates. We've learned that estate planning isn't merely a legal chore but a profound act of love—a legacy woven into our family's narrative. It's about protecting our children, ensuring their well-being, and leaving behind a legacy beyond financial assets.

In conclusion, this journey has been about more than legalities and financial strategies. It's been about the enduring impact of intentional choices on those we hold most dear. Thank you for joining me on this exploration, and as we navigate the vast sea of life, may your legacy be one of love, foresight, and a secure future for generations to come.

All the best to you and your family. May God keep you safe.

Made in the USA
Monee, IL
04 November 2026

67380164R00024